IN THE LAP OF DREAMLAND

(AN ANTHOLOGY OF POEMS)
(PAPERBACK, DECEMBER 2024)

COMPILED & EDITED BY
DR. SONIA GUPTA

DEDICATED TO

DREAMLAND
THE FUN WORLD

CONTENTS

FOREWORD

"Amazing anthology reflecting the beauty of dreamland filled with a mixture of emotions and imaginations, radiated in these verses."

*Here is the impressive international anthology **"IN THE LAP OF DREAMLAND"** compiled and edited by renowned editor, Dr. Sonia Gupta, dedicated to the theme 'DREAMS', featuring poems by acclaimed poets who shared their thoughts and emotions about their dreams. A dream is a pursuit of happiness, an emotional state in which one experiences joy, pleasure, or bliss. Our lives flow between reality, dreams, and reality in a dream. Desires and fantasies drive us forward.*

The poems of the anthology introduce us to a world of dreamland where man is a bird with joyous wings, spinning on his toes, dazed by freedom, his heart singing in the flight of the captivating breeze. Feelings erupt fiery. The authors see dreams as our thoughts flowing like a river. We expect desires and fantasies to be positive and directed in a progressive direction from the development of life.

Poets advise us not to lose hope when longings are not fulfilled. Life has positive and negative sides. Your mistake may be right to me and unacceptable to others. Longings lead us forward with impulses of faith, and life becomes more meaningful and positive. Dreamers offer new solutions and transform reality. Some wishes come true after years. Poets advise us to be brave, have big dreams, painting golden paths and possibilities. A dream is a step forward, an urge and inspiration, a projection into the future.

Dr. Sonia Gupta is an established multilingual author, poet, editor, reviewer and translator. She edits anthologies, poems, and magazines, writes reviews of poets from different countries, and publishes a monthly electronic poetry magazine "Canvas for Thoughts", dedicated to a theme she sets. Her projects and precise selection of poems - composition, design, editing - are impressive. She designs the title pages herself, adding beauty and charm to the works. My congratulations to Dr. Sonia Gupta and all the poets featured in this volume for their wonderful contribution. Indeed it is an amazing anthology reflecting the beauty of dreamland filled with a mixture of emotions and imaginations, radiated in these verses. I am sure this book will be admired by all readers.

Stoianka Boianova
(Poet, Reviewer & Critic)
Sofia, Bulgaria

You Dream

You who walk modestly on your path,
And hear the heart of the Earth,
And you sense the rotation of the planets,
And you feel the pulse of the stars;
You who are a star inhabitant,
And you want to write with light;
You who have not forgotten,
That we were created in the likeness of God,
And you dream we go back to Paradise,
To be there where we were created for;
You, who ... if you really exist,
And I follow you,
And others if they followed you there,
And others...
We will return to the sacred earth,
We shall be in the dreamed land,
We will be there,
Where the godlike,
Live with the Gods.

© **Stoianka Boianova**

About the Reviewer

She is a poet, writer, author, editor and reviewer. She has authored eleven books: poetry, novel and short stories. and co-authored four bilingual books, poetry and haiku – in India with Minko Tanev. She has participated in over 60 international anthologies and publications with numerous awards and recognitions. She edits dictionaries and books. She is in the European Top 100 of the most creative haiku authors. She won several awards, "First World Poetry Competition of Newspapers and Televisions", 2020, China, Chinese International Zhengxin Poet Award, 2022, International Poetry Prize "Ossi di Seppia", 2023, Italy. She is a Chairwoman of Haiku Club – Plovdiv, an editorial board member of "Haiku Sviat/Haiku World" magazine. She is also a member of PEN Bulgaria, Union of the Bulgarian Writers, the Bulgarian haiku Union, the Haiku Foundation – USA, United Haiku and Tanka Society – UK, the World Haiku Association, Japan, Global Honorary Council of Federation of World Culture & Art Society (Singapore). She is a Physicist and has worked in the field of measurement accuracy - metrology, standardization, certification, authorization.

- **Facebook ID***:*
  https://www.facebook.com/stoianka.boianova.3
- **Email ID***: stboianova@abv.bg*

PREVIEW-1

"Through these verses, let us float in the lap of dreamland to enjoy with our inner self."

*The new poetry anthology **"IN THE LAP OF DREAMLAND"** dedicated to the theme 'DREAMS', compiled and edited by Dr. Sonia Gupta, includes poems by authors from different countries and continents, from far and near destinations with writing constellations. What we have in common is that we are free to dream, floating in our dreamland to jump over clouds - there are no shackles to hold us back. Our dreams are crowned without our attachments. They show us flights, exciting meetings, bring us happiness.*

We connect, we take the form of dreams. In the land of dreams shine the moon rings of love. Dwelling in the land of desires - our thoughts are positive. We are mindful of our distinct mission – to keep dreaming, to turn our longing into reality. Our utopias come alive with the magic of love - we are confident that one day we will survive together. Our loving harmony and sense of unity in wholeness will not be lost. Let hope not leave us, and if it is not enough for us, let us rediscover it in the poems of the presented poets.

May our hearts sing joyfully beyond the horizon outlined and longed for in our prayers. Let's take our step in the direction where our feet lead us. Beyond the limits, as it were. With dreamy wings sprouting. Soared with their imaginations into the ages to come. Truly it is a gift from Above. To be dreamers and poets. With a prayer that God will watch over us.

Dr. Sonia Gupta is an established poet and author of twenty-five independent books, editor of several anthologies, poems and magazines, translator and reviewer. I feel glad to be a part of her projects. Presenting anthologies on meaningful and important themes, she is doing a remarkable job in the field of literature that will be admired forever. Today, again it's my pleasure to scribble my words for her new anthology, **"IN THE LAP OF DREAMLAND"**. *Indeed, it is a wonderful compilation that will touch the hearts of readers, igniting the spark of inner thoughts motivating them to live their dreams with charm and enthusiasm. Through these verses, let us float in the lap of dreamland to enjoy with our inner self. My congratulations to Dr. Sonia Gupta and all the poets for their determined spirit to create this new anthology.*

- Minko Tanev
(Poet, Reviewer & Critic)
Sofia, Bulgaria

Star Alphabet

*Our celestial proto-language
echoed in dark, empty rooms
I was a star dweller and a mystic -
I did not stop my dreaming.*

*And here I am on the ground
with the cosmic ideal -
I have chosen a homeland
and the aliens in me are tossing.*

*And infinitely, and without beginning
messages of stellar inhabitants
come to us from the future
from the Akash records.*

© Minko Tanev

About the Reviewer

He is a poet, writer, author, editor and reviewer. He has authored 6 books and co-authored 4 bilingual books, poetry and haiku – in India with Stoianka Boianova. He has participated in over 60 International anthologies and publications with numerous awards and recognitions. He has edited over 70 books. He is in the European Top 100 of the most creative haiku authors. He has won several awards, "First World Poetry Competition of Newspapers and Televisions", 2020, China, Chinese International Zhengxin Poet Award, 2022, International Poetry Prize "Ossi di Seppia", 2023, Italy. He is a member of Union of the Bulgarian Writers, the Bulgarian haiku Union, the Haiku Foundation – USA, United Haiku and Tanka Society – UK, the World Haiku Association, Japan, Global Honorary Council of Federation of World Culture & Art Society (Singapore). He is a Philologist - Bulgarian language. He was a lecturer of Bulgarian language for foreign students – Medical University, Plovdiv.

Facebook ID: https://www.facebook.com/minko.tanev.9
Email ID: minkotanev@abv.bv

PREVIEW-2

"Beautiful anthology full of joy, passion and determination weaved by one's mind in the embrace of dreams."

Our dreams are stories and images that our minds create while we sleep. They are still an enduring source of mystery to scientists and psychological doctors today, trying to unlock those age-old questions, why do we dream? What causes them? What do they mean? There are lots of explanations which include the representation of desires and wishes, processing information gathered throughout the day as well as working as a form of psychotherapy and interpretation of random signals from the brain and body during sleep. The content and function of dreams have been topics of scientific, philosophical and religious interest throughout recorded history. Dream interpretation was practiced as far back as the third millennium BC by the Babylonians and earlier by the ancient Sumerians. The dream starts in the mind, exists in the mind, and with ambition and persistence, it can be carried to its dreamland through and achieved, giving a sense of accomplishment and fuelling one to move forward in their life.

*Taking "Dreams" as the central theme of this anthology, Dr. Sonia Gupta has again come up with a new collection of endearing poems **"IN THE LAP OF DREAMLAND"**. The anthology consists of fifty poets from around the world, each of whom has penned beautiful and unique poems about dreams and what they mean and represent to them. Each one is wonderfully expressive in its words, imagery and passion. Amazing are these dreamers, these artists, these creative souls that stretch the imagination's very boundaries.*

*Dr. Sonia Gupta has already edited numerous anthologies and write-ups of different poets and authors throughout the world. This current anthology **"IN THE LAP OF DREAMLAND"**. is yet another achievement for her as an Editor. A renowned author of 28 independently published books in English and Hindi, she is making her mark on the pages of literature with her contributions. I am very honoured to be a part of her projects, for which I wrote previews. This for me has been and will continue to be very memorable. I am truly amazed by the way she accomplishes her tasks before the given time. Presenting different poets from different regions on a single platform and providing them with the opportunity to contribute to literature altogether is an appreciable effort made by her. I congratulate her on another beautiful anthology that is full of joy, passion and determination weaved by one's mind in the embrace of dreams. I am sure this book will be well received and enjoyed by its readers. May everyone's dreams come true, dream BIG my friends!*

-Donna McCabe
(Poet & Reviewer)
Rhondda, South Wales, UK.

Enchantment

As I close my eyes and drift off to sleep
I see the land of enchantment
Where love greets my feet
A magical world that's forever exciting.

A spectrum of colour
Forever inviting
So many journeys to have
So many different people to be.

Tonight, what to do
Where should I go
Then you show up and at once I know
A mission in black.

This friendship is forever
You're my best friend
You were there from the beginning
And I know you'll be there at the end.

© Donna McCabe

About the Reviewer

She is an established poet with over 20 years of experience whose vast variety of work has gained her multiple accolades within her field of literature over the years. From being published in journals, magazines and anthologies as well as being a highly respected admin in multiple social media groups, she is a regular contributor to literature. Besides this, she is an artist also. Her intricate wordplay displayed in her works has been personified by her past and concurrent experiences which include her hardships, trials and tribulations. Her lifetime admiration of reading and writing and love of art has steered her into an adventurous new direction of collaborations with an up-and-coming Canadian artist Ala Ilescu whose idiosyncratic mind and artistic works compliment the vivid images her narrative works paint. These collaborations have resulted in a beautiful book of poetry and artwork entitled "Explosion of Love" published on Amazon. Her creativity has also taken her onto other platforms in recent times, Using Instagram to reach out and display her love of writing, artwork, and love of the natural world to a wider audience. Her writings and interactions with the wider poetry communities there have helped her gain a good following and many features and awards.

- **Email id-** *donna_salisbury@sky.com*
- **Instagram page -***@donnamccabe_*
- **Facebook page-** *Poemsbydonnamcc*

PREFACE

God has gifted us with a wonderful life, full of adventures, joy, pains, achievements and many more. Our most unique blessing is our mind, which weaves infinite thoughts to form a cobweb in which we all get caught. Out of our daily routine, night is the most favourable period for spending time with ourselves. Away from the crowd of the world and all chaos, we get lost in our DREAMLAND, where countless DREAMS embrace us. Amazing is this separate world that takes us to a new life full of vivid experiences. DREAMS are actually the reflection of our past and envision of our future. They either make us or may break us too. And the amazing thing is that nobody knows from where they come and where they go, nobody of us knows. Their mystery is really beyond the limits of understanding. Whatever it is, DREAMS are our true companions making us aware of happenings in our future and motivating us to grow further.

*We have published several anthologies on different themes to date. Continuing that journey, a thought came into my mind to bring a new anthology dedicated to DREAMS. And the current anthology **"IN THE LAP OF DREAMLAND"**, in your hands is the result of that thought. It is a compilation of 50 poems composed by 50 poets from around the globe. Through these poems, poets have expressed the different thoughts and emotions they experience while floating in the lap of their DREAMLAND, when they are all alone in their embrace. For some, DREAMS bring joy and passion, for others, they bring fears and tears; variable feelings. Reading these verses inspired me to keep this title of the current anthology **"IN THE LAP OF DREAMLAND"**. Contributions by many budding young poets have added more beauty to this anthology. These poetic souls are for other poets and writers.*

As an Editor, I had a huge responsibility on my shoulders to select the poems, compile, edit and design this anthology. I have tried my best to accomplish my job. Here, one thing I would like to highlight is that the role of editing regarding punctuation, commas, capitalization of the first letter, etc. is excluded from my side because different poets had their own assumptions and not everyone was happy to follow a common rule. So, the poems have been placed as per the choice of the poets. For any plagiarism, editor is not responsible, poets have submitted their poems along with declaration. The entire anthology has been designed by me, including the cover page. The picture on the cover page has been taken from internet resources. Though I am an artist and wanted to paint it myself, owing to some health issues, it was not possible this time. I appreciate the timeless contribution, dedication, and cooperation shown by the poets from day one until the end of this project. I congratulate my entire team, including the poets and reviewers for their wonderful contributions. Let us cherish our DREAMS floating IN THE LAP OF DREAMLAND.

- Dr. Sonia Gupta
(Editor)

ACKNOWLEDGEMENTS

To accomplish any task, there are many invisible hands behind which shower abundant blessings, motivating us to achieve our destination. In the same way, in completing this book, I have been blessed and encouraged by so many for whom I am GRATEFUL by my heart.

First of all, I thank the Goddess of knowledge and wisdom, Maa Saraswati, who gave me the strength to complete this work and encouraged me to pick up my pen to compile, edit and prepare this anthology. In the world, everything changes, but one thing that never changes is our parents. Heartfelt thanks to my parents for their faith in me and showering their infinite blessings on me. Special thanks to my father, who has left this materialistic world to attain the embrace of the divine Lord. He had been my inspiration and will be forever, and his teachings illuminate my life's pathway like an enlightening candle. Thank you Mom, for being there throughout my work and for all your support and blessings.

A huge bundle of thanks to all the authors and poets, who have put in their endless efforts by contributing their wonderful poems that represent the theme of this anthology. Most of the poets are much more senior than I am, and I pay my respect and honour to all of them for their full cooperation from day one of this project until the very last moment, respecting my guidelines.

A token of thanks to the poet 'Stoianka Boianova' from Bulgaria for writing a wonderful foreword for this anthology. Thank you for all your blessings and support. My gratitude goes out to the international poets 'Minko Tanev' from Bulgaria & 'Donna

McCabe' from the UK for taking out their valuable time to write the previews for this anthology despite their busy schedules. Thank you both of you, your words have beautified our anthology.

A word of thanks to all my respected teachers who always showed me the right path in my life and brimmed my heart with their blessings. A lovable token of gratitude to my brothers, sisters and all family members for their love and support always. My regards and love to all friends, far and near. Special thanks to all children of the world to whom we have dedicated this anthology. Last but not least, it will be unfair if I forget to thank the Notion Press publishers, through whom the publication of this book has become possible. Thanks to the entire team for the cooperation. Thank you, readers, fellow poets and friends, for all your love and appreciation.

Dr. Sonia Gupta
(Editor)

MEET THE EDITOR

Dr. Sonia Gupta (Dera Bassi, Mohali, Punjab, India)

Dr. Sonia Gupta is a poet, writer, author, reviewer, editor and translator. She writes in English, Hindi, and Punjabi languages. By profession, she is a Dentist (MDS) with a major specialisation in Oral and Maxillofacial Pathology. She writes in vivid genres of literature like poetry, stories, essays, letters, songs and many more. She has established herself as a renowned author after getting her 28 solo books published to date, of which 11 are in English and 17 are in Hindi. Her English books are poetic collections entitled 'Spectrum of Life', 'Canvas of Life...with My Pen', 'Fountain of Inspirations', 'Meeting My Soulmate', 'Silent Verses', 'Mysterious Musings of Life', 'Agony of Life', 'Miracle of Virtues', 'Acrostic Motivations', 'There is No Darkness' and 'In the Embrace of Love'. Her first English novel is coming soon. Her Hindi books include 16 collections of poetry entitled 'Zindagi Gulzar Hai', 'Ummid Ka Diya', 'Kabhi Jalte Kabhi Bujhte Chirag', 'Kuch Ankahe Ehsas', 'Prkriti Ki Gungunahat','Ujale Tumhare Hain', 'Chhappan Pushpmalaen Kanha Ko Arpit', ' Shaym Ka He Dhyan Kar', 'Jeevan Ka Aadhar Tum', 'Bhajo Madhav, Bhajo Keshav', ' Bahut Priy Naam Govinda' "Kanha Ke Hm Sb Aabhari", "Sharan Aaye Tumhari Hum", "Nman Tumhe Hai Shri Jag Palak", " Hmari Aas Hain Madhav" & " Jai Ho Madhv Tumhari" and one collection of stories entitled 'Aadmi Bne Rehne Ka Dhong'.

Her literary journey continues with a great endeavour. She has gone through many ups and downs in her life that have directed her vision towards suffering and she expresses that with her pen. Her writings reflect her closeness to nature, life, spirituality and humanity. For her, poetry is a God-gifted boon, and she wishes to fly high wearing the wings of poetry. She has contributed to more than 100 national and international English anthologies so far. She is a regular contributor to various national and international magazines, newspapers and journals. She has translated many poems by other poets into English, Hindi and Punjabi languages. She runs a blog about the Punjabi translations of English poems by different poets throughout the world. She is the chief-editor of two online e-zines, **"CANVAS OF THOUGHTS" & "BHAV GAGAR"** *in English and Hindi languages respectively. Her first poetry book in the Punjabi will be published shortly. She is an active member of various literary and creative platforms and has won several awards in writing competitions organised by these platforms. She won a 'gold and silver medal' in a Poetic World Cup contest held by Nigeria in February and May 2018 respectively, the 'Prasanna Jenn Memorial Award 2018' by the Asian Literary Society, and '5th place in the international essay writing competition on skin complexion discrimination' organised by the Literary Society of India in March 2018. One of her essays, 'Our role and responsibilities towards nation', was selected in a national essay writing competition and is part of the book 'Youth as Nation Builders.*

She is a famous name in Hindi literature, too. She writes poems, songs, ghazals, stories, essays, letters, articles and vivid forms of Hindi compositions. Besides her seven independent Hindi books, her Hindi writings are part of several international and national anthologies, newspapers, journals and magazines. She has won many awards for her Hindi writings. Her many projects are underway.

Besides poetry, she is also fond of painting, singing, cooking, knitting, designing, stitching, embroidery teaching and reading, She has won many awards in art competitions. Many of her paintings have been placed on the cover pages of various magazines. Even she herself designed the cover pages of her two English solo books entitled "Fountain of Inspirations" and "Canvas of Life...With My Pen". She is actively contributing to literature via her literary YouTube channel, Facebook page, blog, and Instagram page.

Born and brought up in a family of well-educated people, Dr. Sonia is living her life with simplicity and a mission to do something meaningful. She considers her family her biggest inspiration, as they have always motivated her in each and every phase of her life. She feels proud to have such grandparents who have enriched their children and grandchildren with ideal virtues and morals. Her grandfather is retired from the Indian Army and serves selflessly for society till today, even at the age of 97, and believes in doing his tasks on his own. Her grandmother left this materialistic world in 2020. She was a homemaker, who not only taught her Hindi language since her birth but also made her capable of learning other skills like cooking, knitting and embroidery. Dr. Sonia lost her father, Late Sh. Devinder Kumar, in April 2019, who retired as a Government English Lecturer. He lived his entire life for his children's bright future, and it is his efforts that have led Dr. Sonia and her brothers achieve their goals. As a teacher, he was a renowned name in academics who guided a number of students who are working in well-recognized positions in society today. She is living her life following his teachings and footprints. Her mother, Mrs. Nirmal Devi, is retired as a private secretary from the Higher Education Department. Panchkula, Haryana. She is her best friend, who has always motivated and accompanied her in her every adventure, whether related to her profession, passion or personal life. Dr. Sonia feels fortunate to get two younger brothers, who have always stood beside her in even the darkest phases of her life, encouraging her to move ahead. She considers them the pillars of her life. One of her brothers works as a project manager at USA based company in Houston, Texas, USA. and the youngest one is acting as a manager in the MARTUI company, Manesar, Gurugram, Haryana. He is a professional singer and is training his 9-year-old son in classical music. She feels happy to have her bhabhi like her younger sister, who has always been her best companion. She feels blessed to have many teachers who not only taught her professional skills but also appreciated her passionate ventures and today they also clap for her achievements. As a person, she is a less talkative, simple, humble, hard-working and determined personality. She prefers to utilise every single moment in doing something meaningful rather than wasting it in gossiping. She loves to work in a disciplined and organised way. She has completed her many poetry books while travelling to her work place. She is a deep believer in God and a great devotee of Lord Krishna. She is a member of the 'Mahila Mandal Sangeet Samiti' of many temples in her region and frequently participates in various religious events where she sings religious songs composed with her own pen. Her many religious books are in the process of publication.

Dr. Sonia Gupta is a renowned name in her professional field, too. She is working as an Associate Professor in the Oral Pathology Department at a Dental College near her home town. Recently, she has earned a fellowship in Forensic Odontology under Indian Board of Forensic Odontology. She serves the community by providing dental care. She has several scientific publications in PubMed and Scopus-indexed national and international journals with first authorship, and many more are under review. She is also working on three textbooks of dentistry. She is acting as a reviewer of various medical and dental journals. She actively takes part in various conferences, workshops, community health programmes and events and has presented several research papers and posters. She is a dedicated academician with the goal of making her students excel in their subjects and in developing their multitalented skills. She is enjoying her professional as well as literary journey, which is full of passion and mission.

- ***ADDRESS-*** *#95/3, Adarsh Nagar, Dera Bassi, Dist: Mohali, Punjab-140507, India.*
- ***MOBILE-*** *6280420736*
- ***FACEBOOK ID -*** *100004964983747@facebook.com*
- ***FACEBOOK PAGE -*** *https://www.facebook.com/sonia4840/*
- ***BLOG -*** *http://drsoniablogspot.blogspot.in/*
- ***PUNJABI TRANSLATION BLOG -*** *http://passionatepunjabijourney.blogspot.com/*
- ***E MAIL*** *-drsoniagupta82@gmail.com.*

LIST OF POETS

IN THE LAP OF
DREAMLAND

(An Anthology Of Poems)

(Paperback, 1st Edition, DECEMBER 2024)

Compiled & Edited By
Dr. Sonia Gupta

DREAMS

1. In the Lap of Dreamland

O' when the sun sets in the dusk welcoming gloomy night,
So many dreams my eyes cherish embracing sleep tight,
Forgetting the whole world, I get lost in my dreamland,
Amazing is that moment, away from all tensions.

I touch those twinkling stars, moon and sun,
I dance like a butterfly on blooming petals in the garden,
Becoming a fish and shark, I float in the blue ocean,
Aha! Dressed like an angel, I reach beautiful heaven.

I meet the prince of my life, whispering love words,
Drinking the cup of love, I feel blessed with my beloved,
Sometimes like a child, I play with a teddy bear,
Floating paper boats in the drizzling pitter-patter.

I thread a garland of peace and love in the veil of night,
My heart gets brimmed boarding a magical flight,
So blissful I feel and never wish to open my eyes again,
IN THE LAP OF DREAMLAND, dreams play a game.

© Dr. Sonia Gupta
(Editor)
Title Poem

2. Mysterious Dreams

O' from where they come, to where they go?
Their mystery none of us exactly know,
Embraced in the sleep so tight,
They play magic in the lap of night.

Sometimes they bloom our life into a garden,
Like humming butterflies, we caress petals, leaves and stems,
Sometimes floating in a joyful ocean,
We dance and smile brimmed with joy and passion.

Sometimes they bring us a gloom of despair,
All around nothing seems to be fair,
Life seems to be a hell, a curse and a burden,
We get enclosed with worries and tensions.

Amazing are these dreams and their mystery,
With their magical wand, they build up a story,
When eyes get opened and their euphoria is lost,
Ah! We start laughing as if we had met a ghost.

© Abhishek Gupta

About the Poet

Abhishek Gupta
(Gurugram, Haryana, India)
abhi.4870@gmail.com

He is not a regular poet but writes with passion in his leisure time. He writes in English, Hindi & Punjabi languages. He is also fond of music, singing, art and playing badminton, cricket and chess. Holding a degree in B-Tech (Electronics), he is working as a manager in Maruti Suzuki company at Manesar. He is also a professional singer, with his own YouTube channel. He actively participates in various creative and literary events and has received numerous awards for his skills and talents.

3. Rekindling Dreams

There's many a friend with many a churn,
Their despair is truly a gnawing concern,
What wipes their tears and brings in cheer?
An ear to hear and one's doubts clear,
And glide into light and away from fear.

The hand to help another learn,
His ABCs or ways to earn,
The mind to help another heal,
From his mental squeal or bruises from life's wheel,
The heart that aids to rekindle dreams,
That lights the globe and brings in beams.

Knowing that your dreams are sublime,
Won't these on your goals' list become prime?
Your past baggage won't you discard and climb?
Won't your zeal and zest melodiously chime?
Won't Oneness and Peace then be a matter of time?

© Ambika Gibikote Tadipatri

About the Poet

Ambika Gibikote Tadipatri

(Sydney, Australia)
ambikaprasaddoo@gmail.com

She is a poet, playwright & writer. She writes in the English language. She is associated with various literary and creative platforms. Her work has been featured in several national and international magazines, journals, newspapers and anthologies. She has received many awards for her write-ups. She is also passionate about classical dancing, drama and scriptural studies. Holding multiple degrees and certificates, currently she is working as an English educator.

4. Thanks for Everything

Thanks for everything,
Today and tomorrow,
O' my dreams!

For inspiring me,
For guiding me,
For motivating me.

For turning impossible into possible,
Creating a miracle,
Unbelievable.

Thanks for being,
Always my companions,
When there is none.

© **Amit Kumar**

About the Poet

Amit Kumar

(Ambala Cantt, Haryana, India)
Amit123@gmail.com

He is an 11-year-old budding poet studying in 6th grade. He writes in English & Hindi languages. He is also fond of reading, art and singing. He actively participates in various creative events organized by her school and other organizations. He has received many prizes for her creativity. He is passionate about literature.

5. I Yearn

Sun, stars and moon
Clouds, breeze
Meadows, valleys
Mountains…

Flowers, leaves
Rivers, oceans
Lakes, ponds
Deserts…

All come in
My dreamland
Every night
I yearn to touch them all in reality.

© *Anna Ferriero*

About the Poet

Anna Ferriero

(Torre del Greco, Italy)
annaferriero71@yahoo.it

She is a bilingual poet, writer & translator. She writes in English & Italian languages. She is associated with various literary and creative platforms. Her work has been featured in several national and international magazines, journals, newspapers and anthologies. She has received many awards for her write-ups. She has translated many poems throughout the world into Italian language. She is a representative of Italy in India at Güncel Sanat Dergisi. Currently, she is a student, university researcher and doctor of honoris causa.

6. My Dreams

My little heart
Dares to dream big
Even amidst life's odds
It yearns to take a twist.

My little eyes
Behold big dreams
Even amidst pains
They don't scream.

My little mind
Weaves dreams so complex
Even amidst struggles
It doesn't take rest.

All these are sure
About their dreams
One day, they will turn
Into truth and win.

© Dr. Annie Evangelin. N

About the Poet

Dr. Annie Evangelin. N
(Vellore, Tamilnadu, India)
ann18eva@gmail.com

She is not a regular writer but writes with passion in her leisure time. She has contributed to many literary activities during her academic and professional career. By profession, she is a Dentist with a major specialty in Oral and Maxillofacial Surgery. She has received many accolades in her academics and profession.

7. Dream and Mirror

Love is a dream,
And a dream is a mirror,
You are a mish-mash of,
Mirror and dream.

Through your eyes,
I get my hands,
On a different life's,
Debonair theme.

Your love is like,
Shimmering sun rays,
Twinkling stars,
And moon with its moonbeam.

© Atmaja Mishra

About the Poet

Atmaja Mishra

(Kashinagar, Odisha, India)
prasantmisra87@gmail.com

She is a differently abled budding poet and writer. She writes in the English & Odia languages. She is also fond of art, reading, tattoo designing and music. She actively participates in various creative events organized by different organizations. She has attained multiple certifications in hands. She has a deep interest in literature and wishes to fly high wearing the wings of poetry. Currently, she is in wheelchair, struggling with her disability but she has not left her passion for poetry.

8. Good Things Take Time

Success doesn't come in a day,
A matter of lenience and toil,
No need to stay in turmoil,
Waiting doesn't let you recoil.

Good things filter the best,
Out of all odds and muck,
Each moment to face a test,
Keep dreaming and rock.

It takes time to better the better,
Spring turns up only after winter,
Fetter, not you in the chains of haste,
Keep dreaming and don't let the good be waste.

© Ayushi Pradhani

About the Poet

Ayushi Pradhani

(Balangir, Odisha, India)
pradhaniramesh212@gmail.com

She is a 14-year-old budding poet studying in 9th grade. She writes in the English language. She is also fond of reading, art, dancing and singing. She actively participates in various creative events organized by her school. She has received many prizes for her creativity. She wishes to fly high spreading the wings of poetry.

9. Floating in Dreamland

O Night, let everyone have a sound sleep,
Covering the canopy of dark and silence,
Thou are the necessity of all creatures,
Like a mother, you understand the feelings of others.

Drives to the bed of comfort zone,
What a bodyguard thou are alone,
Makes the world drink the nectar of slumber,
In the compartment of safety inside the heart's chamber.

In your lap, dreams play hide and seek game,
Making us feel the charm of name and fame,
Floating in dreamland, we forget the whole world,
And cherish a mixture of feelings dispersed.

© Ayushman Pradhani

About the Poet

Ayushman Pradhani
(Balangir, Odisha, India)
pradhaniramesh212@gmail.com

He is an 11-year-old budding poet studying in 8th grade. He writes in the English language. He is also fond of reading, art and music. He actively participates in various creative events organized by his school and other organizations. He has received many prizes for his creativity. He wishes to fly high spreading the wings of poetry.

10. A Father's Dream

Trying the best,
Even not spending for himself and for the better half,
At least their children,
Be happy and fulfill their dream.

Want to send children ,
To the best school,
That they can acquire the right skills,
And live a life of their choice.

Try to teach children not to waste resources,
But to prepare for 2050 and beyond,
When greenless earth will be breathless,
That they can live life resiliently.

©Damodar Boruah

About the Poet

Damodar Boruah

(Kakodonga, Assam, India)
damodarboruah14@gmail.com

He is a bilingual poet, writer, author & translator. He writes in Assamese & English languages. He is associated with various literary and creative platforms. His work has been featured in several national and international magazines, journals, newspapers and anthologies. He has received many awards for his write-ups. Holding multiple degrees, currently, he is working as a farmer and Coacher for aspiring students to appear Sainik School and Jawahar Navodaya Vidyalaya Entrance Examinations.

11. They Live On

How many of us have treasured dreams?
Dreams of our loved ones, living or passed away?
Sometimes when we wake up,
We start to pen these dreams,

These dreams may even affect our daily lives,
As they tell a story,
And in many ways,
They transform us into a better person.

We always asked ourselves
Are our dreams real?
All these depend on us
Whether we want all to live on in our lives.

© David Soh

About the Poet

David Soh

(Singapore)
davidsoh.books@gmail.com

He is a poet, writer & author. He writes in the English language. He has authored two independent poetry books. He is associated with various literary and creative platforms. His work has been featured in several national and international magazines, journals, newspapers and anthologies. He has received many awards for his write-ups. He is a high school graduate and currently working as a Financial Adviser Representative.

12. Dreams Are Beautiful

Dreams are beautiful…
If they are positive,
If they encourage prosperity and progress,
Blessings and happiness.

Dreams are beautiful…
If they fulfil our wishes,
Spread love and peace,
Vanishing all anguish.

Dreams are beautiful…
If they make us strong,
Encouraging us to walk,
Even on the thorns.

© Fady Bouaz

About the Poet

Fady Bouaz
(Lebanon, Arab)
boazfady@gmail.com

He is a bilingual poet & writer. He writes in English & Arabian languages. He is associated with various literary and creative platforms. His work has been featured in several national and international magazines, journals, newspapers and anthologies. He has received many awards for his write-ups. Currently, he works as a carpenter and freelance writer.

13. In Search of Fresh Air

How can I live
When severe air pollution
Cripples the lives
For difficult to breathe?

Everything is alright
Even living life in styles
3Ps: Power, Position, 'Paisa'
But it's far more difficult to live.

Fresh environment thousand km far
On the bank of the mighty river
Where ducks playfully swim
Nature's beauty is called 'life actual'.

God has given to all the same
Some have freedom
Some battling for daily demands
Some have all but 'freedom less'.

© Glory Shikha Boruah

About the Poet

Glory Shikha Boruah
(Kakodonga, Assam, India)
damodarboruah14@gmail.com

She is a 17-year-old budding poet studying in 11ᵗʰ grade. She writes in the English language. She is also fond of reading, painting, dancing and singing. She actively participates in various creative events organized by her school She has received many prizes for her creativity. She got the inspiration of writing from his own father "Damodar Boruah" who is a poet. She wishes to fly high spreading the wings of poetry.

14. Dreams & Memories

My life evolves from my nostalgic past,
Of which I recall my school days flowing so fast!,
I was amazed by Ms. Susheila, my teacher at school,
Of whom I was intimidated but listened to every tule.

I thought I would recall tears and laugh with a sigh,
I never thought I look at my laughter and cry,
I never realized I would follow Ma'am like the herd,
In retrospect, I honed my keenness in the written word.

In my memory, Maam encouraged us to read library books,
Wondering does one needs reading when one has sparkling looks,
I think of the school bell, sports and every feature,
My past merged with my present as I became a teacher.

My school years are remembered as I pass memory lane,
Knowing that beautiful nuggets of nostalgic memory joyfully remain,
All my dreams turned into memories,
I cherish them all without any worries

© Heera Nawaz

About the Poet

Heera Nawaz

(Bengaluru, Karnataka, India)
nawazheera@gmail.com

She is a poet & writer. She writes in the English language. She is associated with various literary and creative platforms. Her work has been featured in several national and international magazines, journals, newspapers and anthologies. She has received many awards for her write-ups. Holding an M.A. (English), currently, she is working as an educator and freelance writer.

15. Dream of My Heart

Nestled deep, in the depths of my heart,
Is a dream of the purest joy,
A dream of freedom from sorrow & death,
A dream nothing can destroy.

A dream of when there will be no pain,
Or a loss of love's sweet connections,
A place where we're surrounded by peace,
With no more war and degradation.

A dream, where there are no more cries,
From endless sad and homeless souls,
Where there are bountiful tables of food,
And no more empty bowls.

May all these dreams come true someday,
And the world as we know it, disappears,
So peace for all can reign supreme,
And endless happiness and cheer.

© Kathy Jo Blake-Bryant

About the Poet

Kathy Jo Blake-Bryant
(Bates City, Missouri, USA)
kathyjopoetree@gmail.com

She is a poet, writer & author. She writes in the English language. She has authored four independent poetry books. She is associated with various literary and creative platforms. Her work has been featured in several national and international magazines, journals, newspapers and anthologies. She has received many awards for her write-ups. She is a high school graduate and currently, working as a Domestic Engineer and enjoying her passion of poetry.

16. Beautiful Flower

O' my baby!

In my eyes
I behold
Only your dreams.

I had seen
Only your dreams
Since long.

And I am
So happy
To find you today with me.

You are
The beautiful flower
Of my dreamland.

© **Dr. Kinza Qureshi**

About the Poet

Dr. Kinza Qureshi
(New York, USA)
kinza309@gmail.com

She is not a regular writer but writes with passion in her leisure time. She has contributed to many literary activities during her academic and professional career. By profession, she is a Dentist with a major speciality in Prosthodontics. She has received many accolades in her academics and profession. She is also fond of reading, listening to music and photography.

17. My Best Companions

When the whole world sleeps,
I am awake,
Embracing my dreams,
None of them is fake.

They make me laugh,
They make me cry,
I can express everything to them,
I don't feel shy.

They are my best friends,
My best companions,
Taking away my,
All pains and tensions.

© Lynsey McCabe

About the Poet

Lynsey McCabe
(Rhondda, South Wales, UK)
donna_salisbury@sky.com

She is a 14-year-old budding poet studying in the second year of comprehensive school. She writes in the English language. She is also fond of reading, art and music. She actively participates in various literary and creative events organized by her school and other organizations. She has received many prizes for her artwork and poetry. She got the inspiration for writing from her own mother, 'Donna McCabe'. She wishes to touch the heights of poetry.

18. In Your Embrace

Come! Come !
Oh my dreams,
Night has arrived,
Let us get united.

In your embrace,
I feel joyful,
Blissful ,
Sometimes fearful.

Yet I love you a lot,
Abundant of emotions you have brought,
Within my mind,
Soul and heart.

© Manmohan Rohilla

About the Poet

Manhoman Rohilla

(Gurugram, Haryana, India)
rohillasahab9050@gmail.com

He is a 21-year-old budding poet studying in his final year, at Government Polytechnic. He is passionate about poetry and music. He writes in English & Hindi languages. He actively participates in various literary and creative events organized by his institute and other organizations. He has received many awards for his creativity. He wishes to go for a mile in the field of literature.

19. Last Night

Last night…
I saw a dream
Of meeting
My prince…

We had danced together
Laughed together
Walked together
Sat together…

Weaving so many
New dreams
For our
Tomorrow…

Alas! morning arrived…
My eyes opened
Everything was over
I realized it was only a dream.

© Meena Panchal

About the Poet

Meena Panchal
(Faridabad, Haryana, India)
meenapanchl224@gmail.com

She is a 20-year-old budding poet studying in final year at Government Polytechnic, Faridabad. She is passionate about poetry and fashion designing. She writes in English & Hindi languages. She actively participates in various literary and creative events organized by her institute and other organizations. She has received many awards for her creativity. She wishes to go a mile in the field of literature along with her passion for fashion designing and art.

20. Little Sparrow

A little sparrow
Comes
Every night
In my dreams.

Fluttering and jumping
Here and there
With her
Tiny wings.

She has become
My best friend
My buddy
My smile.

© Meher Mathur

About the Poet

Meher Mathur

(Pune, Maharashtra, India)
kshtjpandey879@gmail.com

She is a 6-year-old budding poet studying in 1ˢᵗ grade. She writes in the English & Hindi languages. She is also fond of drawing. She actively participates in various literary and creative events organized by her school and other organizations. She has received many prizes for her creativity. She wishes to fly high spreading the wings of poetry.

21. Amazing Dreams

How amazing,
Are these dreams,
Sometimes make us laugh,
Sometimes cry.

Sometimes take us,
To the heights,
Sometimes,
To the depths.

Till today,
None could understand,
Their meaning,
And existence.

© Muskan Vashisth

About the Poet

Muskan Vashisth
(Faridabad, Haryana, India)
muskanvashisht184@gmail.com

She is a 20-year-old budding poet studying in her final year at Government Polytechnic, Faridabad. She writes in English & Hindi languages. She is passionate about fashion designing and music. She actively participates in various literary and creative events organized by her institute and other organizations. She has received many awards for her creativity.

22. Hold Our Hands

Hold our hands!
Embrace me tight
My dreams say to me
At midnight.

We will fulfil
Your ambitions
Taking you to
Your destination.

My dreams are wonderful
Beyond this world
They have
Their own dreamland.

© Namrata Dubey

About the Poet

Namrata Dubey
(Faridabad, Haryana, India)
nd7578509@gmail.com

She is a 23-year-old budding poet studying in her final year, data basement management. She is passionate about poetry and reading books. She writes in English & Hindi languages. She actively participates in various literary and creative events organized by her institute and other organizations. She has received many awards for her creativity. She wishes to spread positivity through her poetry.

23. Most Favourite Period

Someone asked me
Which is
Your most favourite
Period?

I smile
And reply
Without any
Second thought.

My night…
When I cherish
My dreams
Floating in my dreamland.

© Nibir Neerlov Borah

About the Poet

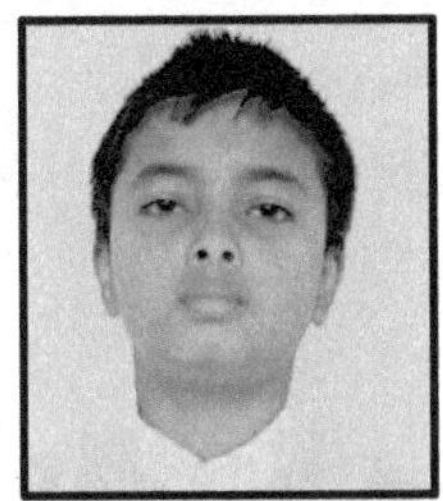

Nibir Neerlov Borah

(Titabor, Assam, India)
damodarboruah14@gmail.com

He is a 12-year-old budding poet studying in 6th grade. He writes in the English language. He is also fond of playing guitar. He actively participates in various literary and creative events organized by his school and other organizations. He has received many prizes for his creativity. He wishes to fly high spreading the wings of poetry.

24. Beyond This World

Beyond this world
There is another world
Full of imaginations
And fantasy.

Where there are
Mixture of feelings
Love, fear, despair, joy
Inspiration and enthusiasm.

This is a world
Of countless dreams
Letting us feel
Something unique.

© Nirmal Devi

About the Poet

Nirmal Devi

(Mohali, Punjab, India)
nirmaldevi@gmail.com

She is not a regular poet but writes with passion. She writes in English, Hindi and Punjabi languages. She is also fond of art, singing, cooking, dancing and knitting. Retired as a personal secretary from Haryana Education Dept. Panchkula, currently, she works as a housewife and social worker.

25. When I Close

O' when I close
My tiny eyes
I fly toward the sky.

Wearing the wings
Of imagination
I fly in my dreamland.

Without any fear
I become
A superman.

I do whatsoever
I wish to do
With a motivation.

© Nishant Gupta

About the Poet

Nishant Gupta
(Gurugram, Haryana, India)
abhi.4870@gmail.com

He is a 10 -year-old budding poet studying in 6th grade. He is passionate about poetry, music and art. He writes in English & Hindi languages. He is also a singer and getting training in classical music. He is fond of swimming, skating, playing badminton, cricket and chess. He actively participates in various literary and creative events organized by his school and other organizations. He has received many awards for his creativity. Recently, he performed as a singer in one of the renowned entertainment shows 'Junior Superstar Season-3' on Sony TV. He wishes to fly high spreading the wings of poetry and music.

26. They Are Still Alive

O' my life has crossed
So many pathways
Met and lost
So many faces.

But they are not lost
Actually
They are still alive
In my dreams.

I still feel
Their presence
Within me
Forever.

© Nishu Kushavaha

About the Poet

Nishu Kushavaha

(Faridabad, Haryana, India)
nishukmri2006@gmail.com

She is an 18-year-old budding poet studying in her 2nd year at Government Polytechnic, Faridabad. She is passionate about poetry and fashion designing. She writes in English & Hindi languages. She actively participates in various literary and creative events organized by her institute and other organizations. She has received many awards for her creativity. She wishes to bring a positive change in the world through her pen and art.

27. Wonderful Alive Dream

It is very hard,
To find true love,
On the earth,
All may not have.

Some are selfish,
Some are greedy,
For a little sacrifice,
Nobody is ready

Love is not for,
Joy or pleasure,
Out of one own pleasure,
One should offer.

It is not demanded,
Or it can't be commended,
It's a wonderful alive dream,
That can never be ended.

© Dr. Okram Shakuntala

About the Poet

Dr. Okram Shakuntala
(Imphal, Manipur, India)
shakuntala.okram@gmail.com

She is a poet & writer. She writes in the English language. She is associated with various literary and creative platforms. Her work has been featured in several national and international magazines, journals, newspapers and anthologies. She has received many awards for her write-ups. Holding a Master in Arts and PhD, currently she works as an Asst. Prof of Economics and HOD, in The Maharaja Bodh Chandra College, Imphal.

28. Dreamland of Love

Leaves me, love, never at that
It levels pegs with my heart
Like no tomorrow ever there was
Sung, I love's link-up cause
Like no one's business - bait
Sing I Love's tranquil trait
Slays me love when see I ways
Something else in night and days-
Feel I find my brightener feet
Never I say right that is it
No matter what I do or speak
Sticks in with me love in pink
In my heart's sure good things
Shines love's moonlit rings
Live I in the dreamland of love lovingly here
Crucial love is luminous dear!

© Prasant Misra

About the Poet

Prasant Misra
(Kashinagar, Odisha, India)
prasantmisra87@gmail.com

He is a bilingual poet & writer. He writes in English & Odia languages. He has authored four Odia and one English poetic collection. He is associated with various literary and creative platforms. His work has been featured in several national and international magazines, journals, newspapers and anthologies. He has received many awards for his write-ups. Holding an M.A. (Odia language and literature), currently, he is working as a journalist.

29. My Only Dream

To become
A
Fashion designer…
Is my
Biggest and
Only dream…
I cherish it
While sleeping
In the lap of
My dreamland…
One day…
It will come
TRUE…

© **Radhika Rohilla**

About the Poet

Radhika Rohilla

(Gurugram, Haryana, India)
radhikarohilla9050@gmail.com

She is a 17-year-old budding poet studying in her 2nd year at government Polytechnic. She is passionate about poetry and fashion designing. She writes in English & Hindi languages. She actively participates in various literary and creative events organized by her institute and other organizations. She has received many awards for her creativity. She wishes to go a mile in the field of literature along with her passion for fashion designing and art.

30. In My Dreams

New hopes
New inspirations
New wishes
New ambitions…

New destinations
New aspirations
New relations
New missions…

My mind weaves
New threads of
New things
In my dreams…

© **Ramanivas Tiwari**

About the Poet

Ramanivas Tiwari

(Sitapur, Uttar Pradesh, India)
ramanivas40@gmail.com

He is a bilingual poet and writer. He writes mostly in Hindi and less frequently in the English language. He is associated with various literary and creative platforms. His work has been featured in several national and international magazines, journals, newspapers and anthologies. He has received many awards for his Hindi write-ups. This is his first English anthology. Holding an M.A. (Hindi), he retired as a teacher and currently, works as a freelance writer and a social worker.

31. Serene Night

Two souls searching for a serene night to mingle with each other.
That ensures their meeting safe and free of cacophony.
The lonely sea shore ecstatic seeing the confluence,
Multiplies the much-awaited dreams of life, one another influences.

Twinkling stars in the azure sky showering flowers of blessings,
Gelid wind whistling piercing but quite appealing,
Rushing sound of serenity in loneliness lustrous heart oozing,
Moonlit busy preparing velvety rosy bed perfume spreading.

Time, space, place splendidly comprehend lover's emotions,
Spell of love makes each other insane in collaboration,
Even in their dreams, they keep their hopes alive,
They are assured that one day they will together survive.

© Ramesh Chandra Pradhani

About the Poet

Ramesh Chandra Pradhani

(Balangir, Odisha, India)
pradhaniramesh212@gmail.com

He is a trilingual poet & writer. He writes in English, Hindi & Odia languages. He has authored six solo books. He is associated with various literary and creative platforms. His work has been featured in several national and international magazines, journals, newspapers and anthologies. He has received many awards for his write-ups. Holding multiple degrees, currently, he is working as a Principal at P S Degree Mahavidyalaya Deogaon, Odisha.

32. I Also Have a Dream

I also have a dream
In my tiny eyes
Which will come true
I have a hope inside.

A dream to become a successful person
To reach my ambition
To fly high beyond the sky
To touch the heights.

To conquer this whole world
To spread love and love
To make this world a peaceful place
To cross every hurdle in life's race.

I know that one day I will succeed
Every war I will win indeed
My dream is my inspiration
To take me to my destination.

© Remy Pandey

About the Poet

Remy Pandey
(Bengaluru, Karnataka, India)
kshtjpandey879@gmail.com

She is a bilingual poet & writer. She writes in Hindi & English languages. She is associated with various literary and creative platforms. Her Hindi work has been featured in several international and national magazines, journals, anthologies and newspapers. She has won many awards for her write-ups. This is her first English anthology. She has a B. A philosophy Honours. Currently, she works as homemaker and freelance writer.

33. Come All of You

Come O' moon
Come' O' sun
Come' O' twinkling stars.

Come O' river
Come O' ocean
Come O' breeze.

Come O' clouds
Come O' trees
Come O' flowers.

Come, all of you
To my dreamland
I wish to touch you all.

© Ritika Kumari

About the Poet

Ritika Kumari

(Ambala Cantt, Haryana, India)
Ritika44@gmail.com

Shi is an 11-year-old budding poet studying in 6th grade. She writes in English & Hindi languages. She is also fond of reading, art and singing. She actively participates in various creative events organized by her school and other organizations. She has received many prizes for her creativity.

34. I Cherish

O' my pen
Moves
Silently
Composing
So many
Compositions
With its ink
Flowing on the paper
In my dreams…
I cherish to be a poet.

© Rivyansh Rohilla

About the Poet

Rivyansh Rohilla
(Dehradun Uttarakhand, India
Rivyansh0312rohilla@gmail.com

Hi is a 12-year-old budding poet studying in 7 grade. He writes in English & Hindi languages. He is also fond of reading, art and football playing. He actively participates in various creative events organized by his school and other organizations. He has received many prizes for his creativity.

35. My Dream Girl

O' I play with
My Doll
Holding her hands
Caressing her curly hair…

I love
To be
With her
In my silence…

She is my
Dream girl
And
Dream queen.

© **Saanvi Gupta**

About the Poet

Saanvi Gupta
(Gurugram, Haryana, India)
abhi.4870@gmail.com

She is a 7-year-old budding poet studying in 2nd class. She writes in English and Hindi languages. She is also fond of singing, playing badminton, skating and painting. She actively participates in various cultural events in her school and has received many prizes.

36. O' My Puppy

O' my puppy
My dear buddy
I love you very much
Even in my dreams…

You are my life
My friend
My rose
My lily…

Come to me
Every night
In my dreams
Without you, I scream.

© Sanchi Kumari

About the Poet

Sanchi Kumari

(Dera Bassi, Punjab, India)
Sunny128@gmail.com

She is a 6-year-old budding poet studying in 1st class. She writes in English and Hindi languages. She is also fond of singing, playing and painting. She actively participates in various cultural events in her school and has received many prizes.

37. Tonight

Love comes to me tonight,
Under the kiss of fond memories,
While the dream falls on my eyes,
I imagine when you held me gently,
In their arms where love and joy were alive.

Like your shadow,
My soul yearns for you,
Spilling thoughts with longing,
On the golden days of passionate love,
When you loved me passionately and madly.

For me, all this wonder,
Your smile, your touch,
Everything I experienced with you,
My nights would be easy now,
And dreams are getting sweeter and sweeter.

© Seadeta Bela Juric

About the Poet

Seadeta Bela Juric

(Bosnia and Herzegovina)
Seadetajurić@gmail. Com

She is a bilingual poet & writer. She writes in English & Bosnian languages. She is associated with various literary and creative platforms. Her work has been featured in several national and international magazines, journals, newspapers and anthologies. She has received many awards for her write-ups. Retired as a teacher, she is living as a housewife.

38. Colours of Dreamland

So colourful
Is the world of dreamland
Full of vivid
Shades and hues…

Every colour
Paints a beautiful picture
To be preserved
Forever in my heart…

Let these colours
Paint my life too
Spreading joy
Forever…

© Shamsher Singh Rohilla

About the Poet

Shamsher Singh Rohilla

(Gurugram, Haryana, India)
shamshers44@gmail.com

He is a bilingual poet & writer. He writes in English & Hindi languages. He is associated with various literary and creative platforms. His work has been featured in several national and international magazines, journals, newspapers and anthologies. He has received many awards for his write-ups. Holding a B.A., currently he works as a Quality Officer in a private company.

39. Wings of Dreams

Wearing the wings
Of my dreams
I fly high
Beyond this world…

I don't know
Where I am
Flying
And why…

I only know
That I cherish
That moment
To the fullest…

And I wish
Never to open
My eyes
Again…

© **Sheetal Kumari**

About the Poet

Sheetal Kumari

(Faridabad, Haryana, India)
skumari06092007@gmail.com

She is a 17-year-old budding poet studying in her 2nd year of diploma in data base management at Government Polytechnic, Faridabad. She writes in English & Hindi languages. She is also passionate about fashion designing & music. She actively participates in various literary and creative events organized by her institute and other organizations. She has received many awards for her creativity.

40. I Was Only Dreaming

The world is a beautiful place
Where all creatures coexist
The ample natural resource
Helps them feed and subsist.

Existence is devoid of strife
And filled with joy and bliss
We play the game called life
With flourish and great finesse.

Where peace reigns supreme
And wealth and prosperity abound,
With no conflicts extreme,
Causing destruction all around.

I smile to myself thinking
Of the seemingly impossible things,
But then I was only dreaming
Of utopia with no attached strings

© Dr. Shyamala Annavarapu

About the Poet

Dr. Shyamala Annavarapu

(Hyderabad, Telangana, India)
shyamala.annavarapu@gmail.com

She is a poet, writer & doctor. She writes in the English language. She is associated with various literary and creative platforms. Her work has been featured in several national and international magazines, journals, newspapers and anthologies. She has received many awards in academic as well as literature. She is a postgraduate in gynaecology and currently, working as a private practitioner.

41. I Thought

In an unusual moment
I thought that
I am the wholesale
Distributor
Of dreams and sole authority of
Ambitions.

From the morning to the evening
There is queue in front of and
Asking for the charming characters.

There I saw
No one without the
Necessity of life and everybody is pleasant and self-reliant
They share the wares they have
And even their dreams.

A world of plenty and sufficient
Where men and materials
Used with utmost care.

© Sreedharan Parokode

About the Poet

Sreedharan Parokode

(Kozhikode, Kerala, India)

sreeparokode@gmail.com

He is a bilingual poet, writer, author & lyricist. He writes in English & Malayalam languages. He has 30 solo poetry books to his credit. He is associated with various literary and creative platforms. His work has been featured in several national and international magazines, journals, newspapers and anthologies. He has received many awards for his write-ups. Holding multiple degrees, he is retired from Calicut University. Currently, he is enjoying his literary journey.

42. You and Me

My heart finds love
My mind finds peace
Even in my solace
When I am in the lap of my dreams.

When none disturbs me
No noise, no chaos
No worry
No pains.

Only me and my dreams
Talking to each other
Creating life's
New chapter.

Steven McCabe

About the Poet

Steven McCabe
(Rhondda, South Wales, UK)
donna_salisbury@sky.com

He is not a regular poet but writes with passion. He writes in the English language. He is also fond of music, traveling, playing football, going gym and having cars. He actively participates in various creative and literary events. He has served in the army for 4 years before leaving and getting married. Currently, he works full-time and takes care of his family.

43. Dreamscape

A gentle breeze hushes the leaves,
Leaves sways shyly,
Moon showers her silver beam,
A sparkling, silvery night.

The river reflects, like a mirror,
A deep silence,
My heart soars like a balloon,
Lost in the moment.

Eyelids droop, shrinking like petals,
Worry- free land,
Butterflies flutter to drink nectar,
A free fair without paying money.

No hindrance for lovers,
Soaring flights of Fancy,
The sun's gentle touch on my lids,
Fades slowly, like ephemeral bubbles.

© Sulochana Narayanan

About the Poet

Sulochana Narayanan

(Palakkad, Kerala, India)
sulsubra@gmail.com

She is a bilingual poet & writer She writes in English & Tamil languages. She has published a solo English poetry book "Imprints". She is associated with various literary and creative platforms. Her work has been featured in several national and international magazines, journals, newspapers and anthologies. She has received many awards for her write-ups. She is also fond of paintings, music and reading. Holding an M.A. (English) and B.Ed., currently, she works as an academician.

44. Different Dreams

When I was a child
My dreams were different
My dreamland was different.

Today when I have turned young
My dreams have changed
My dreamland too.

Now there are
Different thoughts
And perceptions.

Truly said
"Time changes everything"
We have to accept.

© Sunny Kumar

About the Poet

Sunny Kumar
(Dera Bassi, Punjab, India)
Sunny148@gmail.com

He is a 16 -year-old budding poet studying in 11th standard. He is passionate about poetry and music. He writes in English & Hindi languages. He actively participates in various literary and creative events organized by his institute and other organizations. He has received many awards for his creativity. He wishes to go for a mile in the field of literature.

45. Life Is a Dream

The amazing world is my heaven on earth,
I find ecstasy in life on this land of my birth;
My unpredictable life never ceases its mirth.

I'm at ease with dew of the glowing morning,
I enjoy the sensuous delights of the day's tiding;
My life is filled with dreams by night's blessing.

The joys and sorrows of life, I can't transcend,
The strivings of ordinary folk, I can't descend;
Yet, the ridiculous situation, I can suspend.

Life itself is transient, only vision and dream -
The moon, the wilderness of stars — all a dream,
Fleeting life is perishable like a midnight dream.

Life is full of dreams that keep it beautiful…
My truest life is in dreams awake in bountiful,
'Coz, my life is nothing but a dream peaceful.

© Surendra Singnar

About the Poet

Surendra Singnar
(Diphu, Assam, India)

Singnar.s@gmail.com

He is a bilingual poet & writer. He writes in English & Assamese languages. He has authored 2 solo poetry books. He is associated with various literary and creative platforms. His work has been featured in several national and international magazines, journals, newspapers and anthologies. He has received many awards for his write-ups. Retired as a high school teacher, currently, he works as a social worker.

46. Endless Dreams

In the stillness of the deep night,
where the moon whispers her song,
my dreams rise like froth,
to the wind, to time, with no direction.

They are lights that burn in my soul,
drawing worlds of color and peace,
they sing to the rhythm of a calm,
that only the heart knows how to give.

Dreams of flight, dreams of life,
of golden fields under the sun,
where the soul feels no wound,
and the world dances with no role.

In them, I seek an open sky,
a hope that embraces the soul,
and though I may wake in the desert,
my dreams return with the same fire.

© Taghrid Bou Merhi

About the Poet

Taghrid Bou Merhi
(Foz Do Iguaçu, Paraná, Brasil)
taghrid240@gmail.com

She is a multilingual poet, writer, editor, translator and journalist. She has authored 17 books and translated 24 books to date. She is associated with various literary and creative platforms. Her work has been featured in several national and international magazines, journals, newspapers and anthologies. She has received many awards for her write-ups. Currently, she is working as an Arabic language teacher for non-native speakers.

47. I Never Stop Dreaming

One mind stays good, But another feels sad,
Both are close to me and have the same gap.

What they care about me, there is my luck,
They broke in two parts and I am just intact.

How different they are, but I stay as I desire,
When bad, sadness is full, when it is good, pleasure.

In this freak of difference, there is a huge disguised,
The more I break, the more I see wrong. I'm surprised.

Yet I never stop dreaming, yearn to achieve more,
In the lap of my dreamland, I cherish the life at my core.

© Tapas Mahapatra

About the Poet

Tapas Mahapatra
Kolkata, West Bengal, India,
tapasmahapatra025@gmail.com

He is a bilingual poet, writer, author & translator. He writes in Bengali & English languages. He has authored 8 solo Bengali Poetry books. He is associated with various literary and creative platforms. His work has been featured in several national and international magazines, journals, newspapers and anthologies. He has received many awards for his write-ups. He is a Graduate of Calcutta University and currently works as a journalist.

48. Dreams Together

The day
Since
I have met you…

I see
So many dreams
Even with
My open eyes…

It's the magic
Of your love
That I cherish
A paradise…

O' sweetheart!
Let us see
Dreams together
From now onwards…

© Dr. Vaishnavi S

About the Poet

Dr. Vaishnavi S
(Hyderabad, Telangana, India)
vaishnavisecenec@gmail.com

She is not a regular writer but writes with passion in her leisure time. She has contributed to many literary activities during her academic and professional career. By profession, she is a Dentist with major speciality in Oral and Maxillofacial Pathology. She has received many accolades in her academics and profession. She is also fond of travelling and listening to music.

49. I Wish

I sleep
In the lap of
My dreamland
Peacefully and joyfully.

Holding tiny hands
Of my little
And innocent
Baby.

I always wish
This dreamland
Remains the same
Forever.

© **Dr. Vidhya Selvaraj**

About the Poet

Dr. Vidhya Selvaraj
(Chennai, Tamilnadu, India)
dr.rsvidhya@gmail.com

She is not a regular writer but writes with passion in her leisure time. She has contributed to many literary activities during her academic and professional career. By profession, she is a Dentist with major speciality in Orthodontics. She has received many accolades in her academics and profession. She is also fond of travelling, cooking and photography.

50. Strange Dreams

On that dark solitary night,
When the whole world is sleeping,
The one thing that is closest to our eyes,
Are our dreams.

Sometimes, paradise, sometimes, slippery heights,
Sometimes, games and toys, sometimes, take us on flights,
Sometimes, lovable dates, sometimes, prince and princess,
Sometimes, pizza plates, Sometimes, even God and Goddess.

How strange these dreams are,
Everyone is unable to understand near and far,
They themselves bring us joy,
They spread fear and shy.

Dreams are just our thoughts we perceive daily,
And all those imaginations internally,
All those thoughts,
Take the form of those dreams as a whole.

© Vikas Gupta

About the Poet

Vikas Gupta
(Houston, Texas, USA)
Vikas.48@gmail.com

He is not a regular poet but writes with passion. Holding degrees in B-Tech and MBA, he is working as a project manager in one of the multinational companies in the USA. He writes in English, Hindi and Punjabi languages. He is also fond of music, art, cooking, reading, traveling, and photography. He actively participates in various creative and literary events.

51. In My Whole Life

In my whole life,
Many phases I faced,
Some odds, some blissful,
Some sad, some joyful.

People came and went,
Leaving me all alone,
Many a time,
I walked on thorns.

Yet one of my companions
Was always
With me at
Every moment.

My dreamland
Which filled
My heart and soul
With eternal mirth.

© Dr. Vinod Kumar Gupta

About the Poet

Dr. Vinod Kumar Gupta
(Noida, Uttar Pradesh, India)
atalmoradabadi@gmail.com

He is a bilingual poet & writer. He writes in English & Hindi languages. He is associated with various literary and creative platforms. His work has been featured in several national and international magazines, journals, newspapers and anthologies. He has received many awards for his write-ups. His first solo Hindi book is coming soon. Holding multiple degrees, he retired as an Engineer and currently, works as a freelance writer & social worker.

Dreams
ignatianspirituality.com

Edited & Published Anthologies from January 2023 to November 2024

Sweet
Drems

"Our mind cherishes so many dreams in the lap of dreamland. Let this dreamland be alive always to cherish more and more dreams today and tomorrow."

DR. SONIA GUPTA

MAKE WISHES COME TRUE
Dreamland

IN THE LAP OF
DREAMLAND

(An Anthology Of Poems)

(Paperback, 1st Edition, December 2024)

Compiled & Edited By
Dr. Sonia Gupta